THE WORLD
OF JAMES VAN DERZEE

THE WORLD OF JAMES VAN DERZEE: A VISUAL RECORD OF BLACK AMERICANS

COMPILED AND
WITH AN INTRODUCTION BY

REGINALD MC GHEE

Grove Press Inc., New York, N.Y.

We would like to thank the following people, without
whose help this book would not have come to fruition:
Karen Asakawa (research associate); Candice Van
Ellison (technical assistant); Allon Schoener (New York
State Council on the Arts); Thomas P. F. Hoving
(Metropolitan Museum of Art); Lloyd A. Johnson
(Urban Center, Columbia University).

The James Van DerZee Institute, a nonprofit
organization with Mr. Van DerZee as its chairman,
has been set up to further other photographic projects
such as this book.

To all of my people.
—James Van DerZee

To Kathleen and Mary.
—Reginald McGhee

Introduction
by Reginald McGhee

I first met James Van DerZee while on assignment as director of photographic research for the exhibition "Harlem On My Mind" in December, 1967. When I first entered the small cramped studio at 272 Lenox Avenue in Harlem, I was immediately impressed with both the man and his works. This impression has continued to grow as I have gotten to know Mr. Van DerZee and his collection. James Van DerZee made the largest single photographic contribution to the "Harlem On My Mind" exhibition, and his works have brought a tremendous amount of warmth, pride, and true insight into the long neglected history of black Americans.

Mr. Van DerZee began his photographic career in the little town of Lenox, Massachusetts in the year 1900, after discovering that "it was much easier to produce an image with the 'little box' than it was with paints and brushes."

After various jobs in and around Lenox, this young man decided in 1906 to forsake his home town for New York, the original home of his parents. Here he met and married the very beautiful Kate Brown, and shortly after their marriage they spent a year in Virginia. They then returned to New York, where Mr. Van DerZee began a career that was to stretch over six decades, centered primarily in and around the Harlem community.

James Van DerZee was a photojournalist long before the word came into existence. He turned his camera on Harlem's people and events, recording the black affluence of the teens, the heroes of World War I, the so-called Negro Renaissance and the black militancy of the Twenties, the hardships of the Depression, as well as the happier days of the late Thirties. Some famous people photographed by Mr. Van DerZee include: dancer Bill (Bojangles) Robinson; dancer-comedienne Florence Mills; singer Mamie Smith; prize fighter Harry Wills; religious leaders Adam Clayton Powell Senior and Junior, Father Divine, and Daddy Grace; poet Countee Cullen; political figures Chief Edward E. Lee and Ferdinand Q. Morton; as well as two of the best-known names in the world of sports: Jack Johnson and Joe Louis. His photographs of the Marcus Garvey era probably form the most comprehensive essay on this subject. At the same time, he gave just as much attention to the ordinary families who came in for portrait sittings.

Physically, this collection consists of between thirty and fifty thousand prints and negatives, a great many of which are glass plates dating back to Van DerZee's first photographs. It is an amazing feat in itself that these negatives, especially those on glass, have been maintained in such fine condition, some for over sixty years. The size of these negatives varies from the small 2 x 2 inch to the 11 x 14. They are priceless, both for historical and artistic reasons.

I have studied the works of photographers whom I consider to be masters, those who have set the pace and continue to set the pace in this art called photography — people like Steichen, Stieglitz, Hine, Davidson, Hattersley, Bresson, Parks, Capa, Duncan, and Lang—and in my opinion the name of James Van DerZee should be added to this distinguished list. For in this man I have found the same qualities of the masters — an eye for detail, composition, light, form, and texture, and a deep involvement with his subject matter.

In this book of photographs you will not see the common images of black Americans — downtrodden rural or urban citizens. Instead, you will see a people of great pride and fascinating beauty, with a tremendous love for their children. Knowing this man has been a great pleasure as well as an education for me, and I have found in him a dear friend.

Today, at 83, James Van DerZee is still young, due largely to his sense of humor, his keen awareness of the world around him, and his continuous eye for beauty.

James Van DerZee and Reginald McGhee / Photo by Bob Greene

Interview with James Van DerZee (July 3, 1969)

CANDICE VAN ELLISON: We would like to talk a little about your early life. Where were you born?

JAMES VAN DERZEE: I was born in Lenox, Massachusetts, after my father and mother came from New York in 1882 or 1883. They formerly were maid and butler for Ulysses Grant, who at that time was residing at 34th Street, I believe. They came up around the time of the blizzard, to Lenox, Massachusetts, where I was born. I was the second offspring. I had a sister one year older than I, and I had three brothers and another sister. One brother died at the age of six years, and my sister died at fifteen years old in New York. We lived in Lenox until about 1908 I think it was, but I came to New York in 1906. In Lenox I went to public school. I think there were about four other colored families in the whole town, and my father was sexton of the wealthy Trinity Church. We grew up to be Episcopalians. When we came to New York the only people I knew belonged to the Methodist Church, and so I joined St. Marks.

I had two marriages. I was married first by a Baptist minister, Reverend Sims of the Union Baptist Church. In 1915 I started in the photographic business in New York. At that time I did quite a lot of work for the Catholic Church, and I joined the Catholic Church too. So I don't know what I am today.

As I was saying, I came to New York in 1906 and was married and lived in New York for a while and went back to Lenox, but I became interested in photography way back. . . . In fact, all my people were artists and musicians, and my sister was still drawing and painting up to the time of her death. We used to paint a good deal up there, but after I found out there was such a thing as a camera and that you could put people in position and just press the button and you had the picture, then I didn't do so much drawing and painting.

One time I saw a little advertisement in the paper that said that if you sold twenty packages of perfume at ten cents each, you would get a camera and outfit. So I wrote for the merchandise. I guess it took almost two months to sell it because there weren't many people there to sell to, and I had to wait until they used up what they had and then try and sell them again. So after I sold them all the perfume I think I had about two dollars and ninety cents. I took the money in, and the next day I started running to the Post Office and from the Post Office to the Express Office and from the Express Office back to the Post Office looking for this camera and outfit. One day there was a little red card in the box in the Post Office, indicating that there was a package too big to go in the mailbox. My blood pressure must have run up to about 290, I guess, until the man found the package and brought it out. It was about the size of four cough drop boxes all together, and in it were two or three packages — envelopes of chemicals, a developer and clearing solution, and a small box of 2½ x 2½ inch glass plates.

I think there were six plates in the box, and I had two little cardboard trays covered with wax to develop them in. I was never able to make any pictures with that outfit, but I did manage to get the instructions down by heart. I was in the darkroom developing and developing, and one day I saw a scratch across a plate and thought that that must be the picture, but after I brought it out into the light and examined it I saw that there was no picture and that the plate was all black. Later on I managed to get a little more expensive camera, and after that I was always able to make some kind of picture. At the school I went to I made pictures of the class, and the teacher wanted to know how much they were. I said, "Oh, I don't know, about ten cents apiece." So she told me she wanted six of these, and eight of these, and a dozen of those. I was ashamed to take the money, and I didn't make up the pictures because

I was ashamed to take the money. As a matter of fact, I didn't even know that people made a living taking pictures at that time. There were no camera stores there, or studios, but there was a man who used to come around once in a while with a camera and take pictures. He had one picture that I still remember, taken down in the backyard. My mother and my father, and my sisters and brothers and I and the cow were all lined up, and then the man said it was too dark to make pictures that day and he would have to come back some other day. So we made another appointment and he came back. I don't know what became of that picture, but he was the only one who was taking pictures around there. If I had known at the time, I could have made a good living. Besides, I knew most of the wealthy people in the town, and of course they had large mansions in various spots. There was not much way of reaching them, although I did have a bicycle, but the roads were muddy and hard to ride a bicycle on. But at that time I was photographing such people as the Vanderbilts, the Morgans, and the Westinghouses, the Frelinghuysens and the Parsons and the Lemeers.

As a matter of fact, I have a letter here from John E. Parsons. His daughter was a Sunday School teacher of mine, and I have a letter from his grandson, thanking me for a picture of his grandfather that was used in *The New York Times* about the year 1915, I think. He was the highest-paid counselor at that time. He established the first sugar trust, the first trust company, which was the New York Sugar Trust.

I was married in about 1908 and I had two children. One died at one year old, and another, Rachel, died at fifteen. She used to make very good pictures before she died and also draw and paint and make her own dresses and hats. I did have a picture of Rachel around, I mean some pictures that she made, in some of those books, but I guess they are in storage.

In 1915, my first job as a photographer was in Newark, New Jersey. I applied for a position there. The man advertised for a darkroom man, so I figured I was dark enough to take the job and I applied. I guess he had a different opinion because he said after a while, "Well, I did want someone who could operate, too, and I don't know if my trade will stand for your operating." Well, not knowing his business, I had to agree with him, but he was doing a very cheap type of work — three pictures for twenty-five cents, finish them while you wait. Some of the shop girls used to come in every week and have pictures made. On the Jewish holidays he had to be away, and it was up to me to make the pictures. So I took my time and posed them up and tried to get good pictures of them, and that was something that he didn't do because he was getting so little money for them. I would take time to pose them up, so finally they would come by and they would ask for me, and even when he was there they would look in and see if I were there. They would come by, looking in the door, and he would say, "What do you want? Do you want a picture made? Come in. I will make a picture." "Uh, uh, is the colored fellow there?" So finally he called me out, "Come here, Jimmy, somebody wants you to make the pictures." So finally I was making as many pictures outside as I was developing inside, but he never raised my salary, which was $5.00 a week. But I was anxious to learn what I could and he never knew that I was learning because I immediately saw the system and how he was making them and putting them in the projecting machine and blowing them up to any size from the wet negatives. And after a while I moved back to New York.

VAN ELLISON: I understand that you have lived through four wars. Could you tell us some things that you remember about Harlem during the war?

VAN DERZEE: Well, it looked like everybody was going into the army. They had several classes: Class A, Class One, Class D, Class Two, and C and B, and they were calling them pretty fast. At that time I was really in the picture business. I had a studio on 135th Street near the library. That was in 1916, 1917. Well, the war was on, and the boys used to make some pictures before they went, and afterwards their mothers and fathers would have their pictures made and send them to the boys over on the other side. And when they came back we used to make them in their uniforms. I made one, I remember, of Roberts, the World War I hero. I think he captured fifteen or sixteen Germans with his bare hands, or with grenades. I have several photographs of Roberts and Needham. I made some of both of them together. I believe they're both dead now.

I had occasion at that time to photograph a great many people. Marcus Garvey and his different parades, meetings, halls. Daddy Grace didn't come until considerably later, and Father Divine came along even later. At that time there was a movement that was quite active, and everyone was joining and seemed to be very enthusiastic about it. They were clamoring for some sort of a leader and he [Garvey] came along just at the right time.

I remember one occasion when we made some pictures for some prince who was visiting, Prince Tolo. He got his pictures, and after that he said he was going on a trip and he wanted some more pictures made. He wanted me to make as many as I could, let him take as many as he could with him, and asked me to mail the rest C.O.D. I didn't like the idea very much, but he explained that the rate of exchange was very low and he didn't want to put out any more cash at that time. Anyhow, I did make up about 1,500 pictures and let him take them along with him. I mailed some to Chicago, and they lay in the Post Office for quite some time. Finally the Post Office sent me a notice that they had not been picked up, and then a second notice, and finally a third notice that I had better call for them or they would go to the dead letter office. Then I wrote the Prince and he sent another letter saying that he was going on to the next stop and I should have the pictures forwarded there. That's quite a long story. But to make it short, I finally got paid for them just before he sailed for Europe. I met him at the boat and managed to collect a matter of about $300.00 for the balance of the pictures just before he left, but I had to have him taken to the police station. The young lady who was with him paid for the pictures and off he went.

Then Father Divine came along, but that was considerably later too. I did a lot of work for him in different banquet places. Daddy Grace had quite a place on 116th Street, and I did a great deal of work for him there.

I made Florence Mills' funeral pictures, and as a matter of fact only yesterday I took a picture of the wife of the Borough President's secretary at the same funeral parlor as I made the pictures of Florence Mills. She was laid out in the same place. Florence Mills was taken in 1925.

I also have photographs of Powell, and also Bill Robinson, the Norfolk Kids, Sam Langford, Harry Wills, Jack Johnson, and I photographed, what is the boy's name, the one who married the beautician? Can't even think of his name now.

VAN ELLISON: Joe Louis.

VAN DERZEE: That's it, Joe Louis. Well, that's how I know I'm getting old. People you've been calling by their names all along. It's like these Everready pencils. They write in some places and in others they don't. You figure things, and all of a sudden it goes out of your mind and you get no response.

But it has been very interesting. I like music very much, and I was doing music before I got into the picture business.* Then they started building gramophones and phonographs and victrolas. Then, when the radios and TV came along I knew they weren't going to need any more musicians because I could see them fading out right there. When I started playing music, why, you picked up an instrument and tooted it and everybody would be looking and looking to see where it came from. After they started building radios, you could have a hundred-piece orchestra playing and they wouldn't even bother to look to see where it was coming from. But I played for many dances. The last job I played was with Fletcher Henderson. It was a private

*Mr. Van DerZee plays the piano and the violin — *Ed.*

affair. We used to go out playing on Long Island and in road houses, and I like music much better, but I found out that I had to eat three times a day and in music sometimes I didn't work three times a week, so I decided to pick up my camera and see what I could do with that.

At that time there were not many studios, but then Eastman started putting cameras in everybody's home and everybody's apartment, and now they've got them so foolproof no one can make any mistakes. So the greatest part of my work in recent years has been making copies and doing restoration work.

VAN ELLISON: Mr. Van DerZee, getting back to when you first started in photography, did you know anything about some of the men who were working during that time, men such as Steichen, Stieglitz or Lewis Hine?

VAN DERZEE: Who are they?

VAN ELLISON: They are all master photographers, especially Steichen.

VAN DERZEE: Oh? I haven't even heard of them today. At that time there were a couple of very good photographers who inspired me. A fellow by the name of Elker, Eddie Elker. I saw a picture of his, of Bessie Smith, in *Esquire* magazine.

VAN ELLISON: How about Carl Van Vechten?

VAN DERZEE: Then there was Walter Baker. He did a good deal of work. He was supposed to have been the most prominent one at that time. He wasn't an artist, but he was a fairly good workman in photography.

VAN ELLISON: How about Carl Van Vechten?

VAN DERZEE: I haven't even heard of him.

VAN ELLISON: He was doing work during the Twenties primarily.

VAN DERZEE: In New York?

VAN ELLISON: Yes, in New York. In Harlem, as a matter of fact. He was there during the time of A'Lelia Walker.

VAN DERZEE: I made some photographs of Madame Walker. Also Madame Washington. The Apex Beauty School had a great deal of work done by me. I used to do all of these graduation classes. Every year or twice a year she would come in from Atlantic City and have photographs made, two or three hundred dollars' worth. I made pictures that went in all the different places in Atlantic City and the different studios that she had around, and I made up large pictures for her to hang in those places.

VAN ELLISON: I know that in 1907 you were down in Virginia near the Hampton Institute ...

VAN DERZEE: Oh, yes. I went down with my first wife to Newport News, Virginia, and we also stayed with some people down in Phoebus, Virginia. At that time I worked at the Hotel Chamberlain and did a little private photographing on the side. We made some pictures of the teachers of the Whittier School, which was a preparatory school for the Hampton Institute. I made some photographs there for the girls on the beach and the teachers. They had costume plays, and I made pictures of them in the school-house and in the classroom. I did a great deal of work on the side down there, but I didn't get very much money for it because I wasn't charging very much, and I made most of the pictures on my own initiative. It wasn't that they ordered pictures.

But when I was at home in Lenox, Massachusetts, I made a great many pictures of the hotel there. Until they opened the hotel I guess, I hadn't seen twenty-five colored people together at one time, but there were a great many colored bellmen and waiters at the hotel. I used to photograph the bellboys and waiters and do a little work for some of the guests in the hotel, and I decided that the following year I would decorate my room and make up a regular studio there. But I had the misfortune to break a dish. I was accused of breaking a whole tray of dishes, although I had only broken one, and there was a contention with the dishwasher, who said I had broken a trayful. And before I knew it he and I had an argument and I was dismissed, so I lost that whole season that I thought was going to be so good.

But still I managed to do quite well with photography. Had I known as much as I do now I could have had quite a fine studio on Fifth Avenue, because I had a very fine clientele at that time. While I was here at Lenox Avenue, at 272, before I was evicted, some people came in and had pictures taken. They were going up to see the doctor next door and they stopped in to have some pictures made. I told them that I would be glad to make them, but the cheapest that I made was three pictures for $2.00, and that would only be one person. They said that they didn't care what the pictures looked like. They wanted the pictures taken all together because one of the boys was going into the Air Force. So I said, all right, maybe you will take my wife up for a ride in an airplane because she likes to go in an airplane. One girl said, "Where does she want to go?" "Not very far," I said, "only out to my home in Lenox, Massachusetts." "Lenox, Massachusetts — who do you know out there?" So she began mentioning a bunch of people that came to Lenox every year. She mentioned one family, and I went to the drawer, in the file next to where I was sitting, and pulled out a letter that was addressed to me from the Hotel Eden in Rome, Italy. The letter said that it was very sweet of me to send those lovely photographs and that I deserved a great deal of credit for taking such good pictures. The letter was postmarked 1902, Hotel Eden, Rome, Italy, and the writer said that she spent the whole day riding in automobiles, which was the height of her ambition. Anyway, as the girl was reading the letter, she was amazed to find that it was from her mother — because I had made pictures for her mother before she — the daughter — was ever born. So they had about fifty dollars worth of pictures made, and a few weeks later I saw in the magazine section of the Sunday *Journal American* that this same girl was married to one of the Carnegie boys, the steel magnate's son. And she was shocked and surprised at the coincidence that she should drop into this little dump, practically in Harlem, and find letters from her mother. She begged me to give her one of the letters, as her mother had died, and I made a copy of it and gave it to her. I had several letters in her mother's writing.

VAN ELLISON: You know, in going through your collection, I have found that you have maintained your negatives almost since you began photography. What made you hang onto these negatives? What made you keep such a file when many photographers that you mention here have long since died and their collections also have long since disappeared.

VAN DERZEE: Well, it seemed as though I had a personal interest in the pictures I made, and I did my best and I tried to make them as good as I could. And if they were satisfactory to me, then I just kept them. Sometimes they seemed to be more valuable to me than they did to the people I was photographing, because I put my heart and soul into them and tried to see that every picture was better looking than the person — if it wasn't better looking than the person I was taking, then I wasn't satisfied with it. And a great many of them used to ask me — perhaps not a great many, but one or two, one girl particularly, I remember she said "Mister, can't you make no pictures that look like me? Everybody says, 'Daisy, that's a good picture but you don't look like that.' Can't you make no picture that looks like me?" I said, "Sure, I can make pictures that look like you. Don't the proofs look like you?" She said, "Yes, but they look so bad," she says. I would retouch the pictures and take out the unnecessary lines and shadows so the pictures would always look a little better than *they* did, and then, before taking them, I would figure out the best angle to try to get as much light and expression and character in the picture as possible, and so they became of interest to me.

Then I began making pictures for calendars, and when people would come in to ask about having pictures taken, I would pose them so that they would be appropriate for a calendar picture, and if it came out satisfactorily then I would get them to sign releases. Then I would submit them to the different calendar houses and for quite a while I made up a great many thousands myself, and I found out that other companies started making calendars of Negro subjects, and I began making pictures for other calendar companies. I found this very lucrative, so I began making pictures for the calendar companies. One man out in Forth Worth, Texas wanted Negro subjects, but he didn't know where to get them so he wrote to the Eastman Kodak Company up in Rochester. They referred him to me somehow or other, and I have kept working for them as well as others in the photography business until I got a mortgage on my place to repair it and make some improvements and the bank gave me commitment papers to take the mortgage.

VAN ELLISON: Mr. Van DerZee, when you began photography around 1900, I know that it was in its infancy. Will you tell me a little bit about what it was like?

VAN DERZEE: Well, the plates were very heavy and they were very frail, and if you dropped one of them, that was it — but you knew no different at that time. The most popular dry plates of film at that time were the Eastman, Hammer, and Stanley, and the speed was about 40. Today they have film way up to 200 and faster than that, 250, and even faster. In those days, you used to have a glass powder called flash powder. It was very good, and in fact I think the flash powder was almost better than some of these flash bulbs today because, as far as illumination is concerned, you could make it as bright as you wanted to. The only trouble was that there was a good deal of smoke afterwards. You would go out and shoot in a hall full of people, and you would use this flash powder and bang! would go the flash powder. The smoke would go all the way up to the ceiling, and before it came down we would try to make a second shot if necessary, because we knew that when that smoke came down all the people were going to start sneezing and coughing and choking.

VAN ELLISON: Flash powder was also a little dangerous too, wasn't it?

VAN DERZEE: Yes, it was dangerous. If you knew how to use it you didn't have any trouble. You could get yourself burned pretty badly, because it was quite an intense heat with a very bright light. With light like that you could even get pictures outdoors at night. As a matter of fact, I did have a bottle of it around at home. I'm keeping it as an antique.

And then they had some that they ignited with caps, with little caps like the boys used in those pistols. That would ignite the powder and illuminate the place. One woman I photographed wanted a picture of the dining room, with a cat. She had the cat up in her arms, and I took the camera up. She was petting the cat, and all of a sudden I told her to smile and bang! went this powder and the cat jumped and it was two days before she could find it. But the powder was too quick for the cat. I got her just the same.

VAN ELLISON: Could you determine in some way how much powder to use?

VAN DERZEE: You get that from experience.

VAN ELLISON: There was no way of knowing, no directions as to how much powder to load for the intensity of the light?

VAN DERZEE: Well, there may have been, but I don't recall ever reading about it. I just experimented until I got the amount I wanted. I used a small amount first. If you got enough illumination then you knew how much to vary it according to the size of the place and the color of the walls and the hangings, and how much reflection there was. And after that you had no further trouble.

VAN ELLISON: So it was all on experiment, then?

VAN DERZEE: Yes. In fact, everything I did was experiment. I never went to photographic school.

VAN ELLISON: You never used a light meter or anything like that?

VAN DERZEE: They didn't even have them at that time.

VAN ELLISON: When you were working outside and weren't using the flash cap and the flash powder, did you have a shutter that you just exposed and then closed with a lens cap?

VAN DERZEE: No, I wasn't using a lens cap outside. Almost all of the cameras I had had some sort of automatic shutter. The speed didn't go very high, and outdoors I suppose I did lose a lot of plates, but I didn't lose very many before I knew what I was doing. Eastman was about the best of the plates at that time.

VAN ELLISON: And how large were these plates?

VAN DERZEE: They came in all sizes. I never did buy any more of those 2½ x 2½, because the camera wasn't any good to start with — a broken piece of lens out of an eyeglass! The better camera that I got was a 4 x 5, and today I could use it to quite an advantage yet. It is as good a camera as it ever was.

VAN ELLISON: What make was this camera? Do you remember?

VAN DERZEE: Well, I bought it from Creightlen Brothers. They had a place there on Chambers Street, and I got it through a mail order. Then I got all the Sears Roebuck catalogs and bought the other camera and some telescopes. About the height of my ambition then was telescopes. I tried to play ball one time and the ball hit me on the finger once and like to broke my finger, and I said that's not for me. So it was back to photography. Then I got another crack in the eye once with one of them baseballs and I said, no thank you. Photographing is a little more genteel.

VAN ELLISON: You also use 11 x 14 glass plates?

VAN DERZEE: I used 11 x 14, 5 x 7, 4 x 5, 6½ x 8½, 8 x 10.

VAN ELLISON: But how could you possibly carry around 11 x 14s? How many did you carry at one time?

VAN DERZEE: Depends on what the job was. I carried as many as necessary and probably a couple of extra ones. Of course they were pretty heavy. On the job I would have to carry ten or twelve 8 x 10 plate-holders, and each one of them held two plates, so they were pretty heavy. With the camera and the tripod and all the other contraptions, I couldn't blame those people for buying these small cameras, but I never admired them very much myself, because a great deal of my success in my work was retouching the pictures. That means I could alter the faces and make them look better than the people, and on the small negatives you could not retouch them so well. But on the big plates you could retouch them and I could see what I was doing, and I made a very nice picture, providing the retouching was done fine enough. Once in a while somebody would say, "What's that scratch on there?" if I had done some hurried retouching, or a proof retouching.

REGINALD MC GHEE: You've seen what is done today in photography, and how it has come such a long way. You see the cameras I use, which are 35mm, but you have also seen the enlargement of photographs today, such as the enlargements that we did in the exhibition, "Harlem On My Mind." What is your opinion of the advances that have been made in photography over the years?

VAN DERZEE: It is really astonishing to see the amount of brilliancy in detail that was kept in those pictures. It was amazing to me because it seems that they didn't lose anything at all, even though they were made more than twice the size. And you had some pictures there that were eighteen feet high and fifty feet long and they seemed to have the same amount of detail as the ones that I had made with small negatives. And I believe you made copies of some of them from prints and not from the original negatives.

VAN ELLISON: So then you think that photography is definitely moving along?

VAN DERZEE: Well, photography is moving along considerably, but as for the type of work that they do today — I fail to see what it's all about.

VAN ELLISON: Mr. Van DerZee, I have noticed that in your collection your first use of color film came about only ten years ago. What about in previous days? You did all hand coloring?

VAN DERZEE: We colored them by hand in oil colors and transparent water colors, and for quite a while I worked with these very satisfactorily. After colored pictures came out people began asking for them. And yet some of them didn't know the difference until it became so prevalent that they began to want that for everything. But they didn't want to pay the price. And it took quite a bit more time to produce a picture in natural color until the natural color Polaroid came out. I never thought they would be out as quickly as they were. I wish I had bought Polaroid stock over twenty years ago. I would be sitting pretty today. Some of the colors, even the hand coloring in some cases, was better than the natural color prints. Some people prefer it because you can get the colors just as you want them, but in some of these natural color pictures the color seems to be exaggerated. I don't know whether that's due to the color or the flash bulb they use or the type of film, but I have never done a great deal of color work. I have some 8 x 10 color shots and some 35mm color shots, but that's about all I did in color. And since then, I haven't been doing very much. As I said, most of my work is restoration, and for that you have to hand color.

MC GHEE: In the last year I think that your work has come to the attention of the public and people who are deeply involved in the art of photography. It began, I think, with the show "Harlem On My Mind," and since then it has grown tremendously. I guess it's amazing that you've been at it so long and it is suddenly coming alive. For instance, I know there was a great exhibition called "The Family of Man" to which your work certainly would have contributed greatly. Yet they missed you in some way when they came uptown to get the photographers. What is your opinion of all the things that have happened to you and your work recently?

VAN DERZEE: Well, at the time when I guess I would have been most successful, the time that I really reached the zenith, was the time I lost the house and studio. If I had stayed there and got my mortgage renewed as I wanted to and built up some new showcases, it would have been quite an attractive display. I had noticed once or twice that the different magazines had photographed the front. *Esquire* magazine photographed my showcase one time. They had color pictures made about six years ago in the June issue of *Esquire*. They had two full pages of my front door and people would come from all over and look at the pictures. Some of the students told the teachers — the photographic teachers downtown — about my pictures. One of the teachers came up to see what was so wonderful about them. And a great many photographers seemed to be interested in them, and so I began to think that there was something about them that they didn't see everywhere.

And then I noticed the different showcases of other photographers and I saw that all of them had the same type of pictures. I posed everybody according to their type and personality, and therefore almost every picture was different. In the majority of studios they just seem to pose everybody the same according to custom, according to fashion, and therefore the pictures seem to be mechanical-looking to me. And so my showcases attracted attention, because I posed them all differently, and I tried to pose each person in such a way that the picture would tell a story.

VAN ELLISON: You were the largest contributor to the exhibition, "Harlem On My Mind," and you saw the show, you saw your work, and after that you got a tremendous call for your work. What do you think about this?

VAN DERZEE: Well, I had no idea. It was particular to me, but I did not know it was of such interest to other people. But I could have given "Harlem On My Mind" a much better selection had I known that it was going to bring the attention it did. Because most of the famous pictures that I would have used I didn't use, and there were other expositions where people didn't want pictures for exhibition. I have given people pictures and they never returned them, and I didn't seem to get even any publicity from them, so I thought that this was just another advertising stunt, and that was all. I was quite surprised that I was compensated in the way that I was for this.

I have a great many pictures that I made up for calendar use; most of them are portrait pictures, and they seem to have created a great deal of attention when I put them in the showcase because, as I said before, I try to get as much life and expression as I can into the picture.

THE WORLD
OF JAMES VAN DERZEE

James' first wife Kate and daughter Rachel, Lenox, circa 1908

James and Rachel

Van DerZee women and nephew Reginald

James and Kate with James' sister Jennie

Elder Van DerZee with sons James, Walter, and Charles

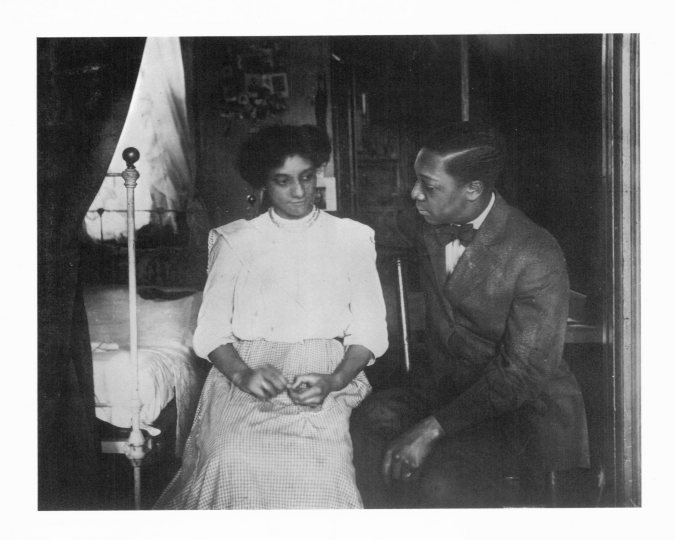

"I shot pictures of my family as they grew
up mainly because they were the most avail-
able subjects around . . ."

Kate, circa 1908

James Van DerZee ⊙ 7

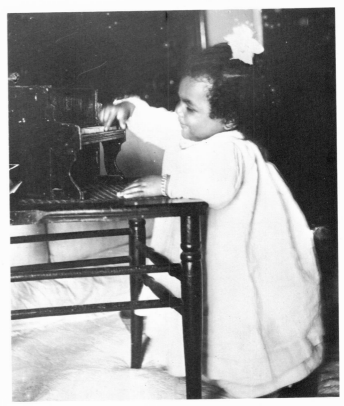

Rachel, circa 1910

James and Walter, 1903, Lenox

Walter and James, 1909

Self portrait, New York studio

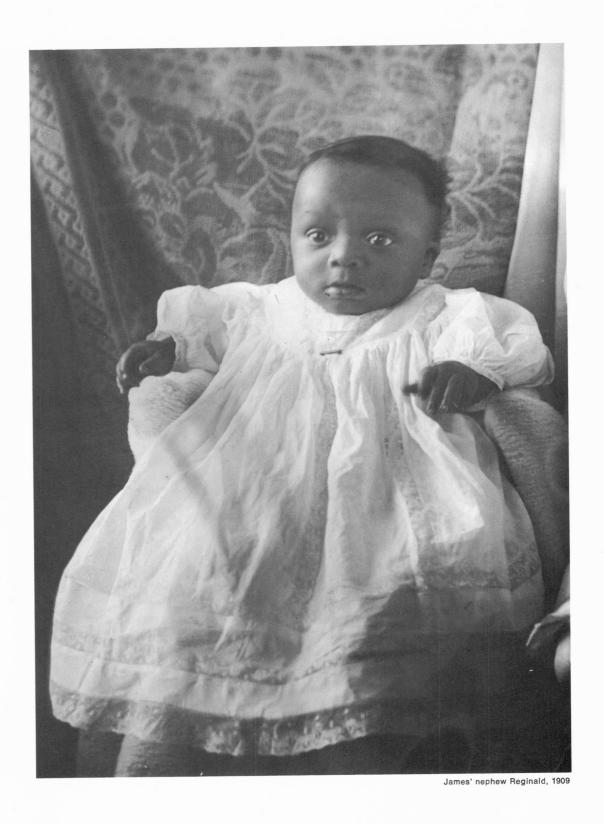

James' nephew Reginald, 1909

Miss Suzie Porter, a cousin, 1914

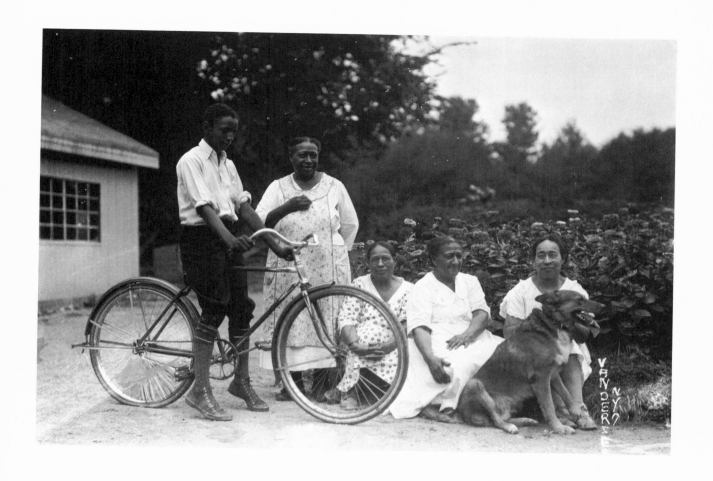

Who did the shirt on the line belong to?

James' aunts, Lenox, circa 1930

James, circa 1930

Walter, circa 1930

James and his second wife Gaynell, circa 1930

"the Institute and the people I lived with in Virginia . . ."

Rabbi Mathews of the Moorish Jews

"My first real customers were the churches . . ."

Daddy Grace

Father Divine

St. Mary's Convent

Reverend Sims of the Union Baptist Church

VANDERZEE
NYC
1925
©46

Rev. Adam Clayton Powell, Sr. and Sunday School class

"Kids make the best subjects. They are so natural and never need retouching..."

Marcus Garvey

"The people were at a loss for a leader..."

Marcus Garvey was born in 1887 in Jamaica. As a
young man he worked as a printer and editor in his
native country and in 1914 organized the Universal
Negro Improvement Association. In 1916 he went to
New York, where he founded a branch of the association and, from 1918 to 1923, edited the *Negro World*,
a weekly newspaper. In New York, Garvey became
the leader of a growing Negro nationalist movement,
of which the chief goal was the establishment of a new
nation in Africa. Garvey died in Jamaica in 1940, and
is remembered today as a man with a vision of unity
and pride for the black people of the world.

Harry Wills

Jack Johnson

Sam Langford

"Three of the great ones . . ."

Chief Edward E. Lee

"The lives of great and ordinary men ..."

Ferdinand Q. Morton

Bill "Bojangles" Robinson

Left: One of the Mills Brothers

Rev. Adam Clayton Powell, Sr. and colleagues

Rev. Adam Clayton Powell, Jr.

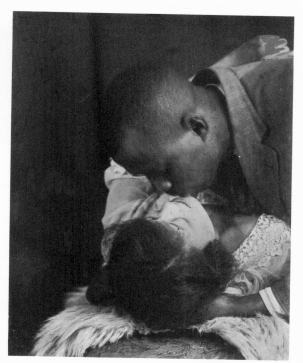

"Women . . . women . . . what can
I say — a lot of beauty . . ."

Florence Mills

James Van DerZee ☉105

Hazel Scott

Madame Walker's Tea Parlor

"I didn't know that money could be made
from pictures, so much of my work was for
the fun of it, and I would give the pictures
away . . ."

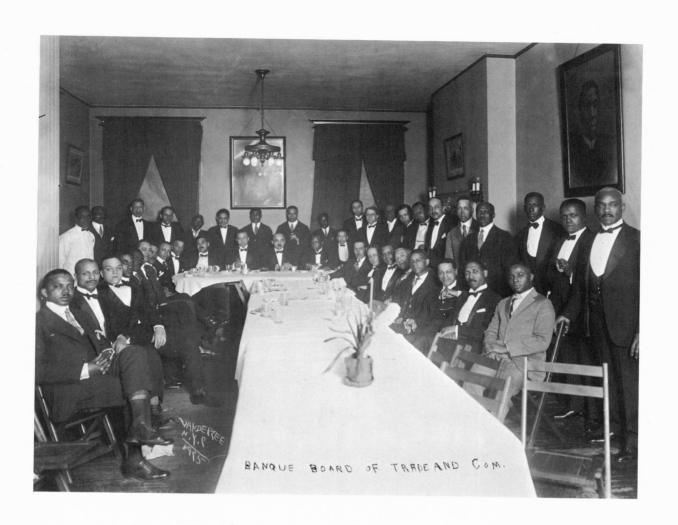

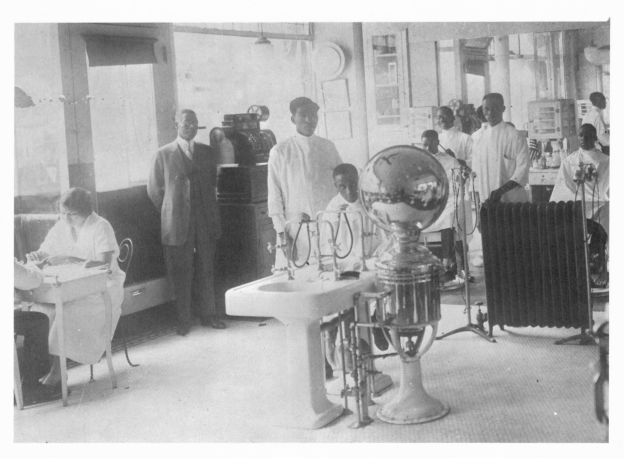

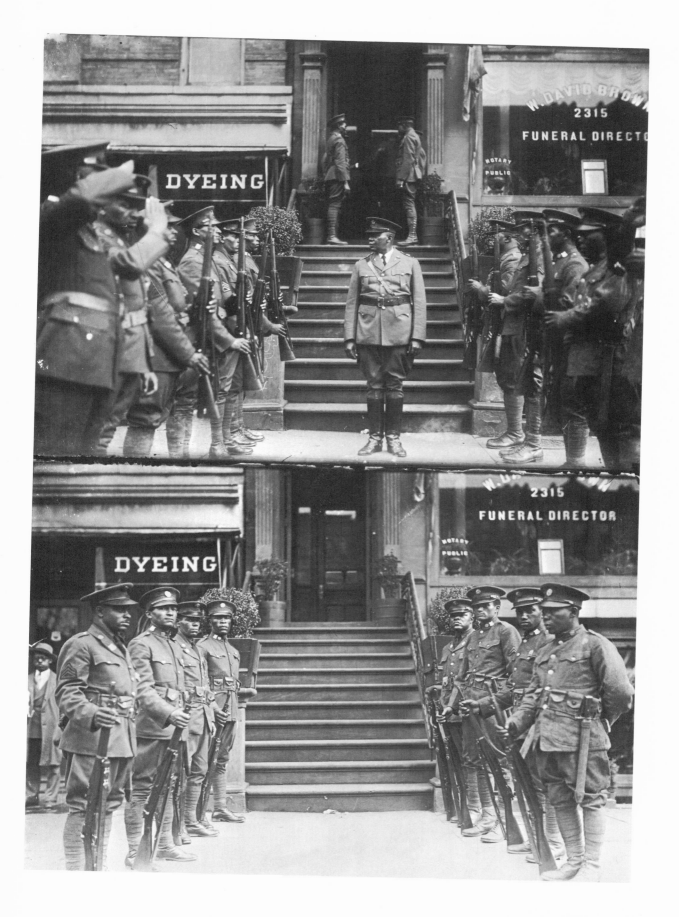

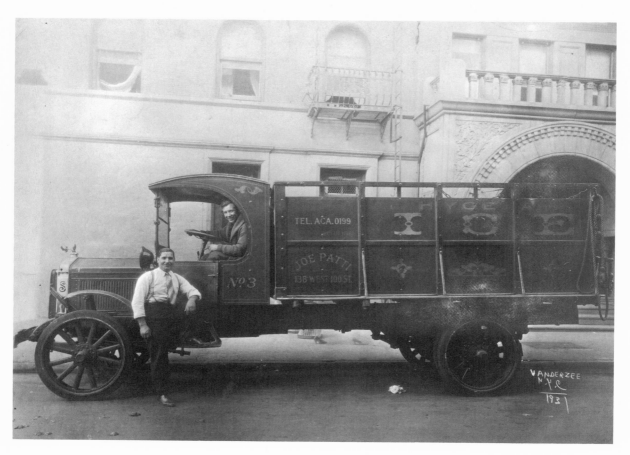

WHEN YOU'RE TIRED YOU'RE TIRED

"With each new camera I would go out and shoot everything in sight . . ."

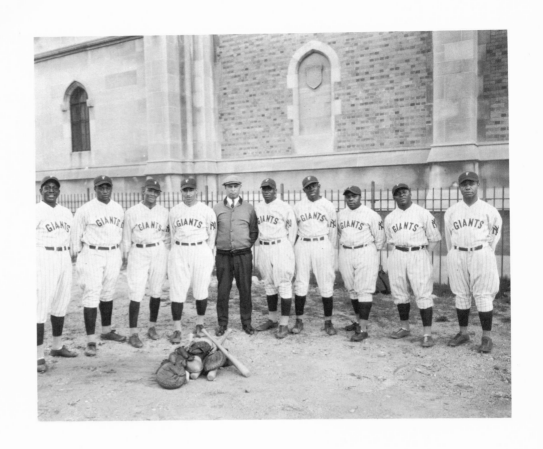